ELEPHANTS

Published by Creative Education, Inc., 123 South Broad Street, Mankato, Minnesota 56001

Printed by permission of Wildlife Education, Ltd.

ISBN 0-88682-226-2

ELEPHANTS

Created and Written by
John Bonnett Wexo

Zoological Consultant
Charles R. Schroeder, D.V.M.
Director Emeritus
San Diego Zoo &
San Diego Wild Animal Park

Scientific Consultants
Charles A. McLaughlin, Ph. D.
Director
San Diego Museum of Natural History

Mark S. Rich, M. S.
Director
Mesker Park Zoo
Evansville, Indiana

Creative Education

Art Credits

Paintings by Barbara Hoopes

Additional Art

Page Eight: Bottom Left, Walter Stuart; **Page Nine: Upper Right,** Walter Stuart; **Page Sixteen: Upper Right,** William Border; **Page Seventeen: Bottom Center,** William Border; **Upper Right,** Karl Edwards; **Page Twenty-Two:** Map by Walter Stuart.

Photographic Credits

Front Cover: Hans Reinhard *(Bruce Coleman, Inc.)*; **Page Ten: Upper Left,** Mark N. Boulton *(Photo Researchers)*; **Bottom Left,** Philip Hart *(Animals Animals)*; **Bottom Right,** Clem Haagner *(Ardea London)*; **Page Eleven: Upper Left,** Alfred Eisenstaedt *(Time-Life)*; **Middle,** Zoological Society of San Diego; **Pages Fourteen and Fifteen:** Patti Murray *(Animals Animals)*; **Page Eighteen: Middle,** Veronica Tagland *(Chess Piece Courtesy of The Norton Simon Museum)*; **Page Nineteen: Middle,** Courtesy of Phillip Sills; **Pages Twenty-Two and Twenty-Three:** Joseph VanWormer *(Bruce Coleman, Inc.)*.

Our Thanks To: Dr. Marilyn Anderson; Charles L. Bieler; Richard L. Binford; Dr. James M. Dolan, Jr.; Dr. David A. Fagan; Ron Garrison; Tom Gould; William Noonan; Michaele Robinson; Philip Sills; Lynnette Wexo.

Contents

2 Months Old

Asiatic Female

Asiatic Ma[le]

5 Years Old

Elephants are the largest of all land animals. And they are among the strangest-looking animals in the world, with their long trunks, big ears and pointed tusks. There are two basic kinds of elephants—African elephants and Asiatic (or Indian) elephants. It is rather easy to tell one kind from another.

Asiatic elephants have smaller ears than African elephants. They have a high forehead with two rather large "bumps" on it.

The back of an Asiatic elephant bends up in the middle, and usually only the males have tusks.

African elephants have very large ears. Their foreheads don't have big bumps on them. The back of an African elephant bends *down* in the middle, and both the males and females have tusks.

African elephants are larger than Asiatic elephants, and the males of both kinds are larger than the females. The average Asiatic

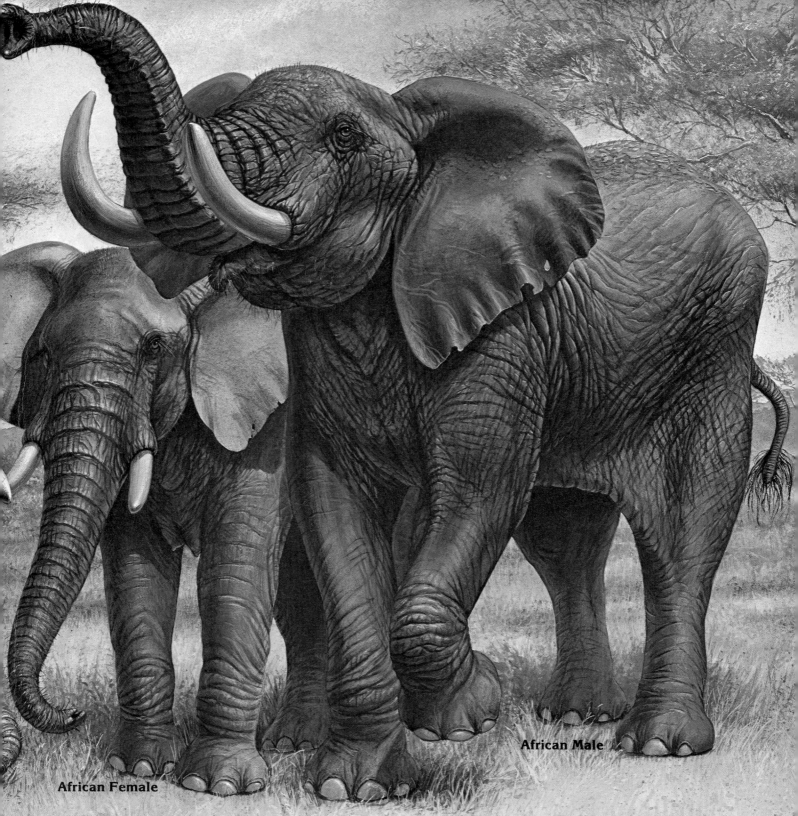

African Female

African Male

male is about 9 feet tall at the shoulder (2.74 meters) and weighs about 10,000 pounds (4,535 kilograms). African males average about 10 feet tall (3 meters) and weigh about 12,000 pounds (5,443 kilograms).

Some elephants grow much larger than this, however. The largest African male on record was over 12½ feet tall (3.66 meters) and weighed about 22,000 pounds (9,979 kilograms). This single elephant weighed as much as *150 average-size people!*

Male elephants are called *bulls* and females are called *cows*. Young elephants are called *calves*. When an elephant calf is born, it is already a big animal. It is about three feet tall (1 meter) and weighs about 200 pounds (90 kilograms). Baby elephants are covered with hair, but as they grow they lose most of it.

Elephants can live a very long time. Asiatic elephants may live as long as 80 years, and African elephants may live 60 years.

For its size, an elephant can move with amazing speed when it wants to. Elephants can run at a rate of 24 miles an hour (38.6 kilometers) for short distances—almost *twice* as fast as a man can run.

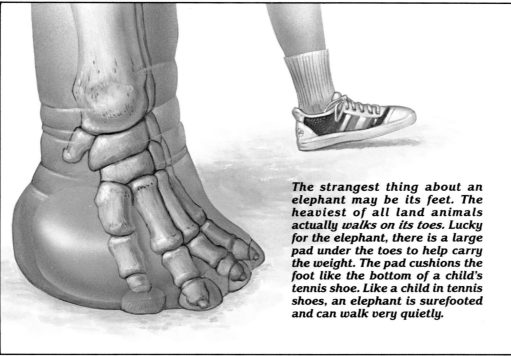

The strangest thing about an elephant may be its feet. The heaviest of all land animals actually *walks on its toes.* Lucky for the elephant, there is a large pad under the toes to help carry the weight. The pad cushions the foot like the bottom of a child's tennis shoe. Like a child in tennis shoes, an elephant is surefooted and can walk very quietly.

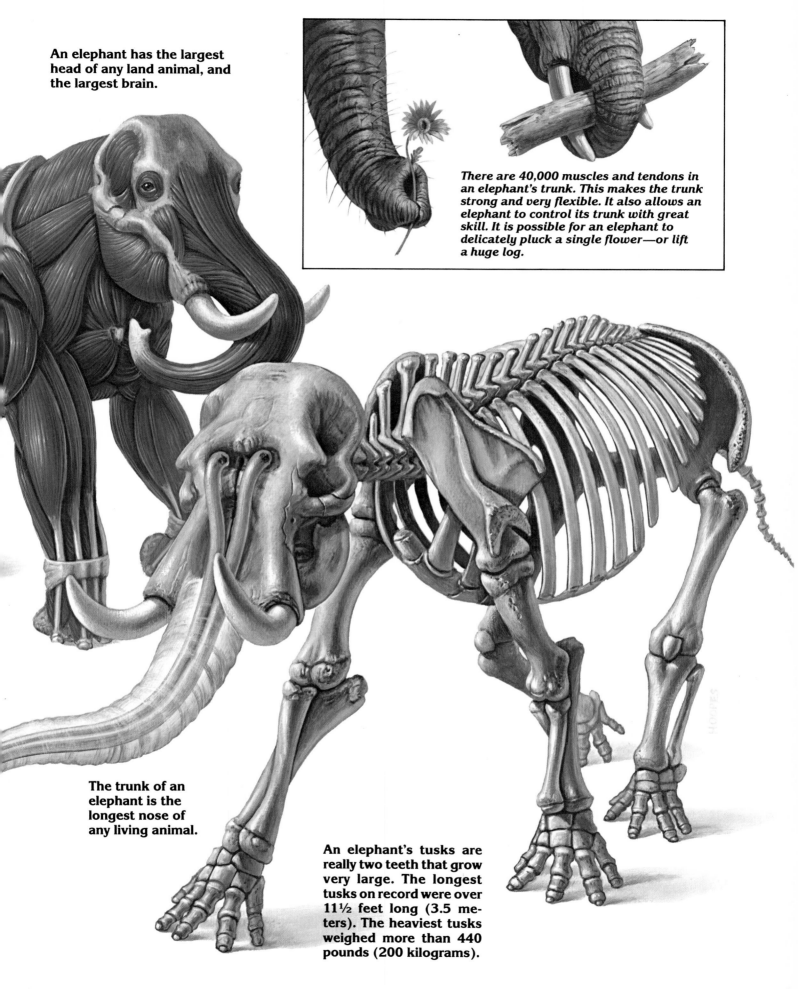

An elephant has the largest head of any land animal, and the largest brain.

There are 40,000 muscles and tendons in an elephant's trunk. This makes the trunk strong and very flexible. It also allows an elephant to control its trunk with great skill. It is possible for an elephant to delicately pluck a single flower—or lift a huge log.

The trunk of an elephant is the longest nose of any living animal.

An elephant's tusks are really two teeth that grow very large. The longest tusks on record were over 11½ feet long (3.5 meters). The heaviest tusks weighed more than 440 pounds (200 kilograms).

It's hard to predict what male elephants will do. One moment they may be gentle and friendly, and the next moment violent and dangerous. In zoos, keepers that work with elephants keep an eye on them at all times. Many keepers say that elephants are the most dangerous animals in the zoo.

The skin of an elephant is thick, but not thick enough to keep bugs from biting. To protect itself, an elephant often sprays dust on its skin. If this doesn't work, the elephant may roll in the mud. This covers the skin with a thick coat of muddy "armor."

Elephants are very social animals. The females and young elephants stay together in a group called a *herd*. The leader of the herd is an old female. Within the herd, the elephants are usually friendly to each other. They often nuzzle each other to show affection.

Mother elephants take very good care of their babies. And the other females in the herd help them to watch out for the babies. Every elephant calf has many extra "mothers" to love it and protect it.

Elephants can make many different sounds, to express their emotions and "talk" to each other. They can scream, trumpet, grunt, rumble and purr. They use their trunks like trumpets to make the sounds louder.

Elephants love water. Sometimes they bathe three or four times a day. They use their trunks to pick up water and spray it all over. The water cools them off on hot days and helps to keep their skin from drying out.

Elephant Ancestors

Elephants have been living on earth for a long time. The first elephant lived more than 45 million years ago. It looked very different from today's elephants. It was only about two feet high (60 centimeters), and it didn't have a trunk. It had tiny ears and its tusks were small. Scientists call this little animal *Moeritherium* (meer-uh-THEER-ee-um).

Since *Moeritherium*, there have been more than *600 other kinds* (or species) of elephants on earth. Most of them have been large with long tusks. But some of them have been small, and some had tiny tusks.

STEGODONT
Stegodon magnidens

HOE-TUSKER
Deinotherium giganteum

STRAIGHT-TUSKED ELEPHANT
Palaeoloxodon antiquus

ANCIENT SOUTHEAST
ASIAN ELEPHANT
Hypselephas hysudricus

ANCESTRAL SHOVEL-TUSKER
Phiomia wintoni

THE FIRST ELEPHANT
Moeritherium lyonsi

CHANNEL ISLANDS
DWARF MAMMOTH
Mammuthus exilis

AMERICAN MASTODON
Mammut americanum

Today, all of these elephants are gone. The African and Asiatic elephants are the only elephants left.

Can you find *Moeritherium* in the picture below? Can you find the Woolly Mammoth, the closest relative of today's elephants? Which elephant ancestor had the strangest tusks?

STEPPE MAMMOTH
Mammuthus trogontherii

IMPERIAL MAMMOTH
Mammuthus imperator

PLAINS MASTODON
Cuvieronius humboldtii

HIGHLAND MASTODON
Cordillerion andium

SHOVEL-TUSKER
Platybelodon grangeri

WOOLLY MAMMOTH
Mammuthus primigenius

13

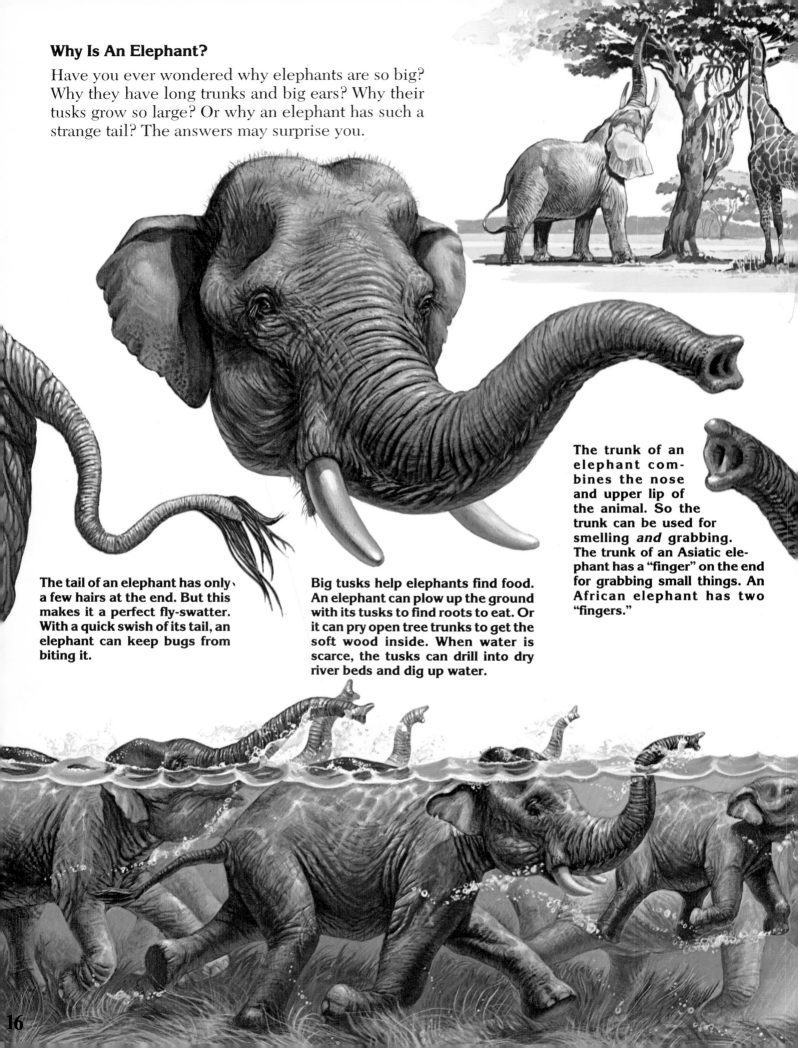

Why Is An Elephant?

Have you ever wondered why elephants are so big? Why they have long trunks and big ears? Why their tusks grow so large? Or why an elephant has such a strange tail? The answers may surprise you.

The tail of an elephant has only a few hairs at the end. But this makes it a perfect fly-swatter. With a quick swish of its tail, an elephant can keep bugs from biting it.

Big tusks help elephants find food. An elephant can plow up the ground with its tusks to find roots to eat. Or it can pry open tree trunks to get the soft wood inside. When water is scarce, the tusks can drill into dry river beds and dig up water.

The trunk of an elephant combines the nose and upper lip of the animal. So the trunk can be used for smelling *and* grabbing. The trunk of an Asiatic elephant has a "finger" on the end for grabbing small things. An African elephant has two "fingers."

16

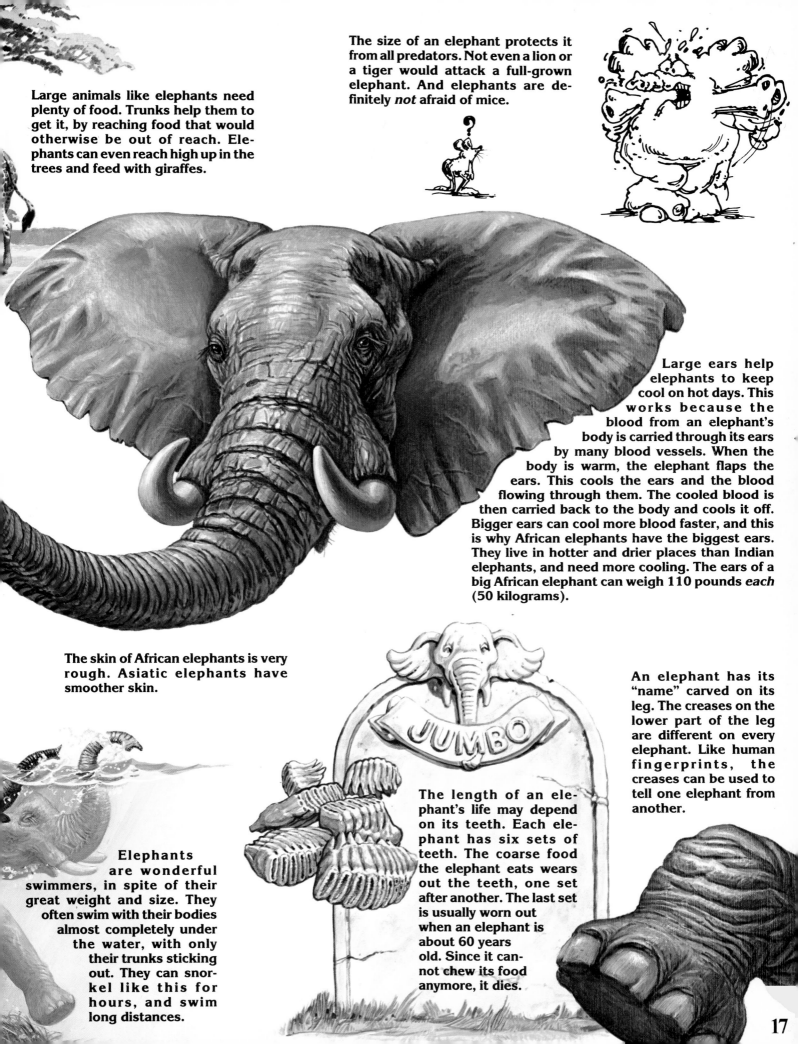

Large animals like elephants need plenty of food. Trunks help them to get it, by reaching food that would otherwise be out of reach. Elephants can even reach high up in the trees and feed with giraffes.

The size of an elephant protects it from all predators. Not even a lion or a tiger would attack a full-grown elephant. And elephants are definitely *not* afraid of mice.

Large ears help elephants to keep cool on hot days. This works because the blood from an elephant's body is carried through its ears by many blood vessels. When the body is warm, the elephant flaps the ears. This cools the ears and the blood flowing through them. The cooled blood is then carried back to the body and cools it off. Bigger ears can cool more blood faster, and this is why African elephants have the biggest ears. They live in hotter and drier places than Indian elephants, and need more cooling. The ears of a big African elephant can weigh 110 pounds *each* (50 kilograms).

The skin of African elephants is very rough. Asiatic elephants have smoother skin.

Elephants are wonderful swimmers, in spite of their great weight and size. They often swim with their bodies almost completely under the water, with only their trunks sticking out. They can snorkel like this for hours, and swim long distances.

JUMBO

The length of an elephant's life may depend on its teeth. Each elephant has six sets of teeth. The coarse food the elephant eats wears out the teeth, one set after another. The last set is usually worn out when an elephant is about 60 years old. Since it cannot chew its food anymore, it dies.

An elephant has its "name" carved on its leg. The creases on the lower part of the leg are different on every elephant. Like human fingerprints, the creases can be used to tell one elephant from another.

People And Elephants

For thousands of years, people have trained elephants and used them to do many things. Elephants have helped people to build cities, to fight battles, and to have fun. In the days before locomotives and automobiles were invented, elephants were the most powerful force available on earth for pushing or carrying things. Asiatic elephants are easier to train than African elephants, so they have helped people the most.

Long ago, elephants were the first "tanks" to be used in war. They wore armor and were used to frighten the enemy.

In our country, important people in a parade usually ride in a big car. In India and other asian countries, important people often ride on a beautifully dressed elephant. They sit in a small house on the elephant's back called a *howdah*. The elephant is guided and controlled by a keeper called a *mahout* (ma-HOOT).

Can you find the *howdah* and the *mahout* in the picture at left? Can you guess why the elephant has blunt covers on its tusks?

18

A long time ago, somebody who had never seen a living elephant probably found an elephant skull. They decided that such a large skull must come from a giant, and the hole in the middle meant that the giant had only one eye. The hole is really the opening of the nose, where the trunk attaches.

Have you ever heard of the *cyclops*—the one-eyed giant that liked to eat people? Did you know that the story of the cyclops was probably started by an elephant skull?

Real Eye Socket

Nose Hole

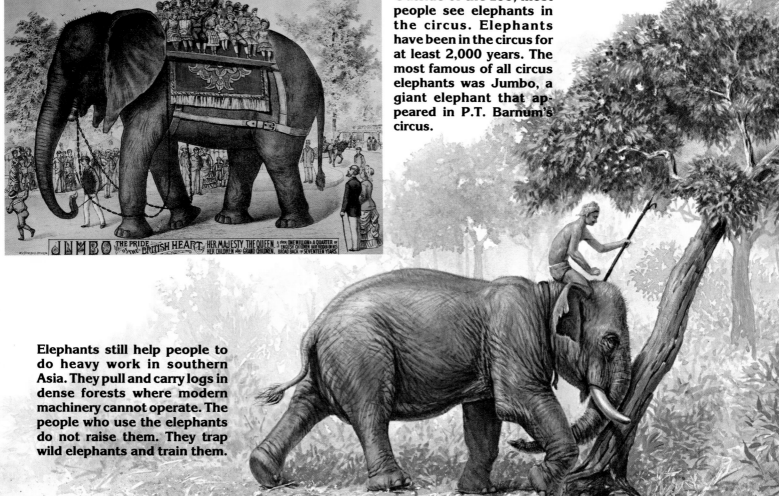

JUMBO THE PRIDE OF THE BRITISH HEART, HER MAJESTY, THE QUEEN, & OVER ONE MILLION & A QUARTER OF ENGLISH CHILDREN HAVE RIDDEN ON HIS HER CHILDREN AND GRAND CHILDREN. BROAD BACK IN SEVENTEEN YEARS.

Outside of the zoo, most people see elephants in the circus. Elephants have been in the circus for at least 2,000 years. The most famous of all circus elephants was Jumbo, a giant elephant that appeared in P.T. Barnum's circus.

Elephants still help people to do heavy work in southern Asia. They pull and carry logs in dense forests where modern machinery cannot operate. The people who use the elephants do not raise them. They trap wild elephants and train them.

A Huge Appetite

Big animals need large amounts of food, and the elephant is the biggest eater of them all. Shown here is the amount of food that one average-sized elephant eats in one year.

In the wild, elephants eat a wide variety of foods. African elephants prefer grass, and under normal conditions 90 percent of their diet is grass. But they will also eat about 100 other kinds of food, including tree bark and fruit. Asiatic elephants live mostly in forests and prefer to eat the foliage of trees and bushes, but they will also eat grass.

An elephant's digestive system is not very efficient. In general, it digests only half of the food the animal eats. As a result, elephants actually eat *twice* the amount of food that their bodies need.

In the course of a year, an elephant drinks 15,500 gallons of water.

Elephants consume large loaves of bread at one gulp —1,600 loaves a year.

Every year, the average elephant eats 100,000 pounds of hay.

12,000 pounds of dried alfalfa add some flavor to the hay.

Minerals and salts are blended into more than 1,500 gallons of mixed grains.

More variety is added to the diet by 2,000 potatoes.

3,000 cabbages, apples, carrots, and other vegetables are provided as "treats."

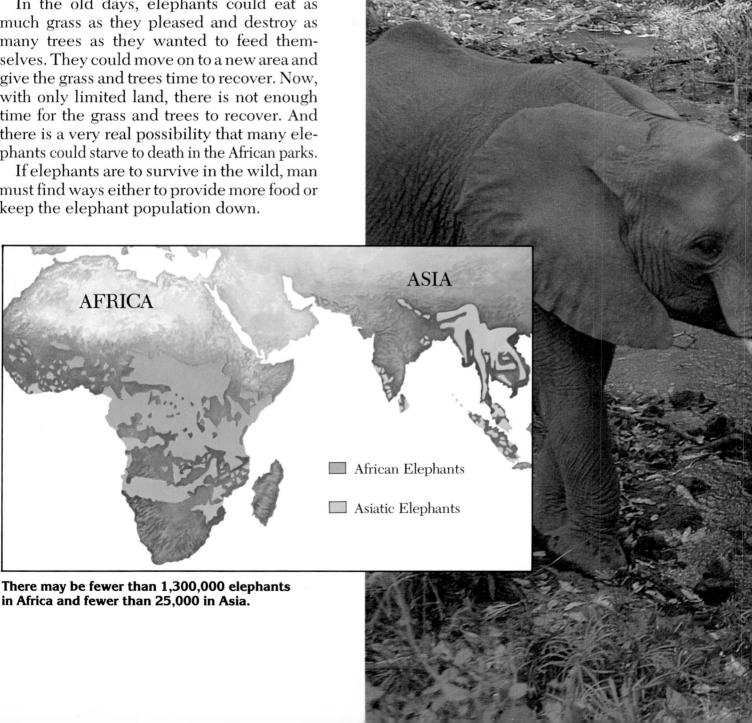

The Future of Elephants Is Up to Us

Elephants have been under attack for a long time. 1,200 years ago, ivory hunters killed all the elephants in North Africa. And by the end of the 19th Century, all the elephants were gone from South Africa.

Today, the price of ivory is at an all-time high. And illegal hunters are a greater threat to the elephants of Africa than they have ever been. But there is an even greater threat—the growing human population of Africa. Elephants have been crowded into park areas that are much smaller than the areas they used to occupy.

In the old days, elephants could eat as much grass as they pleased and destroy as many trees as they wanted to feed themselves. They could move on to a new area and give the grass and trees time to recover. Now, with only limited land, there is not enough time for the grass and trees to recover. And there is a very real possibility that many elephants could starve to death in the African parks.

If elephants are to survive in the wild, man must find ways either to provide more food or keep the elephant population down.

AFRICA

ASIA

◼ African Elephants

☐ Asiatic Elephants

There may be fewer than 1,300,000 elephants in Africa and fewer than 25,000 in Asia.

Index